FIREFIGHTERS

by Golriz Golkar

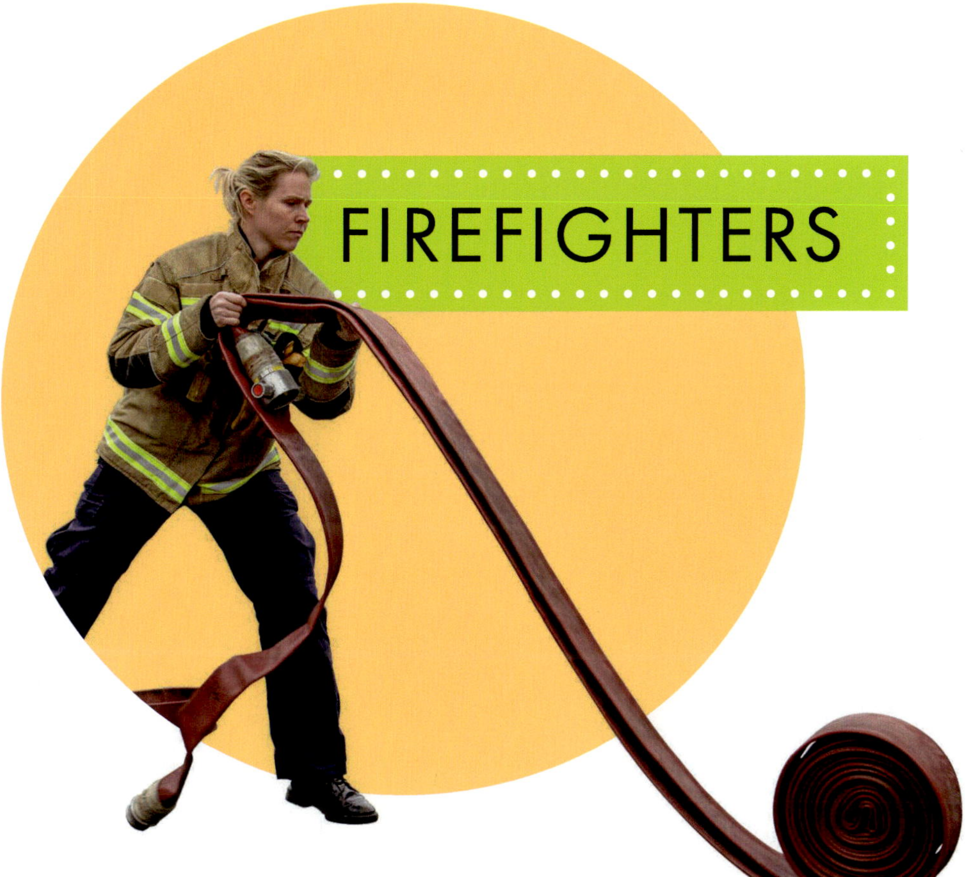

fire gear

fire truck

Look for these words and pictures as you read.

ladder

hose

Firefighters help us.
What do they do?

fire gear

Ring! Ring! Time to go!
There is a fire!
They put on fire gear.
They slide down the pole.

Here comes the fire truck!
Cars pull over on the street.
The fire truck races by.

fire truck

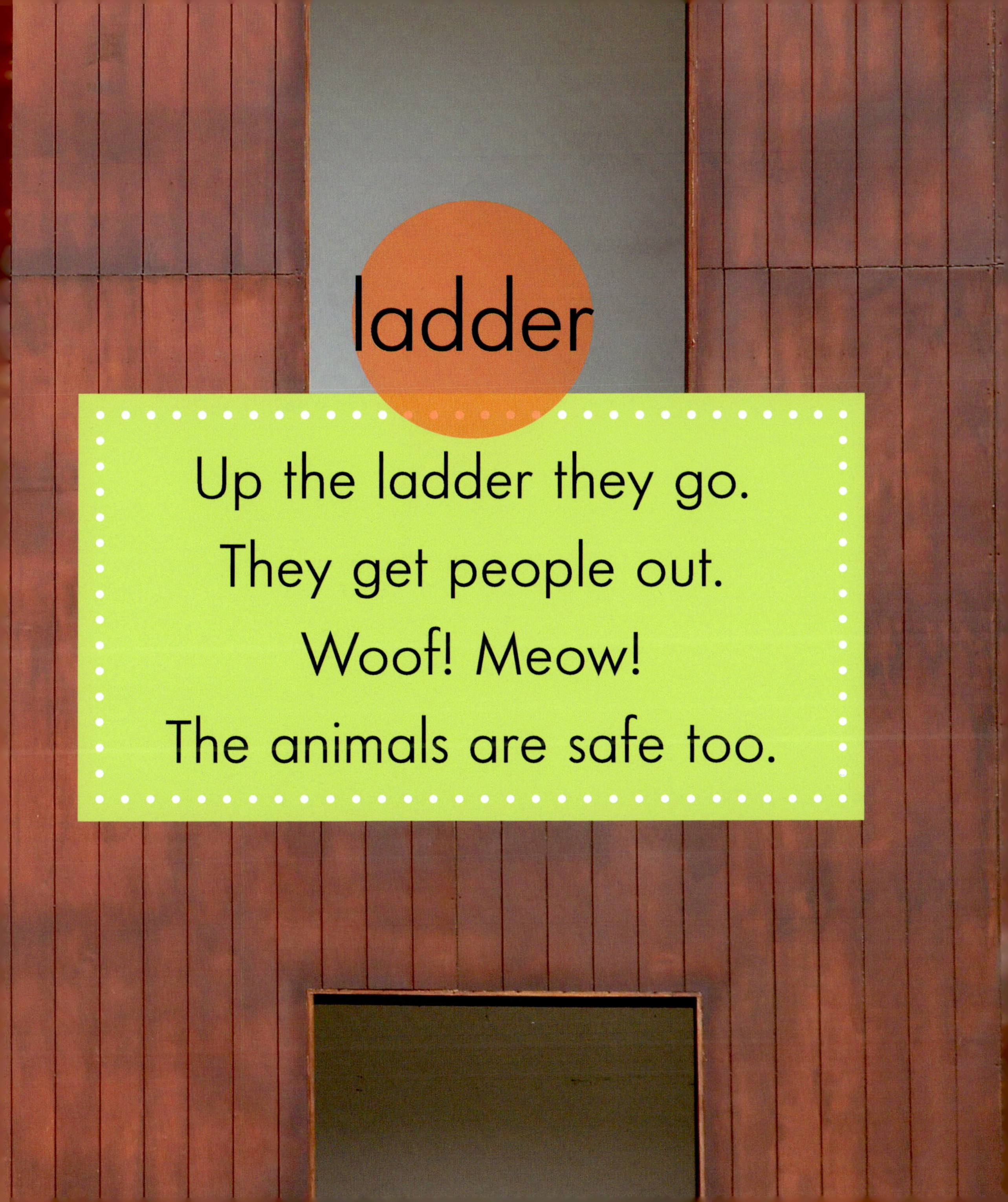

ladder

Up the ladder they go.
They get people out.
Woof! Meow!
The animals are safe too.

hose

Pull out the hose!
Splash!
They spray lots of water.
The fire is gone!

They help people in need.
They give out water.
Sometimes they give hugs.

Firefighters put out fires.
They help keep people safe!

fire gear

fire truck

Did you find?

ladder

hose

Spot is published by Amicus Learning, an imprint of Amicus
P.O. Box 227, Mankato, MN 56002
www.amicuspublishing.us

Library of Congress Cataloging-in-Publication Data
Names: Golkar, Golriz, author.
Title: Firefighters / by Golriz Golkar.
Description: Mankato, MN : Amicus Learning, an imprint
   of Amicus, [2026] | Series: Spot community helpers |
   Audience term: Children | Audience: Ages 4–7 | Audience:
   Grades K–1 | Summary: "Firefighters put out fires, protect
   people and animals, and more. Learn how they help the
   community in this low-level beginning reader that reinforces new
   vocabulary with a search-and-find feature. A great early social
   studies book that will inspire kindergartners and first graders to
   learn about jobs in their community"— Provided by publisher.
Identifiers: LCCN 2024043681 (print) | LCCN 2024043682
   (ebook) | ISBN 9798892004909 (library binding) |
   ISBN 9798892005449 (paperback) |
   ISBN 9798892005982 (ebook)
Subjects: LCSH: Fire fighters—Juvenile literature. |
   Occupations—Juvenile literature.
Classification: LCC HD8039.F5 G66 2026 (print) |
   LCC HD8039.F5 (ebook) | DDC
   331.7/62892—dc23/eng/20250105
LC record available at https://lccn.loc.gov/2024043681
LC ebook record available at https://lccn.loc.
   gov/2024043682

Ana Brauer, editor
Deb Miner, series designer
Sara Hood, book designer
   and photo researcher

Photos by Alamy Stock Photo/Chris
Rabior 911 Images, 10–11, Jeff Gilbert,
1; Getty Images/Frazao Studio
Latino, 14, ryasick, 6–7, Witthaya
Prasongsin, 12, ChiccoDodiFC, 8–9,
Dusan Petkovic, 4–5, serhii.suravikin,
cover, VAKS-Stock Agency, 3